Harry Potter™

CELEBRATORY

EDITION

✶ ✶ ✶

The Best of
Harry Potter Coloring

Scholastic Inc.

An Insight Editions Book

From the orange, brown, and green hues used to convey the warmth and whimsy of the Weasley family to the emerald green and silver of Slytherin house, color was an essential element in bringing Harry Potter to life on-screen and achieving an atmosphere full of enchantment.

Let the film stills, unit photography, and concept art at the back of this book be both guide and inspiration as you explore the color of the Harry Potter films.

GRYFFINDOR™

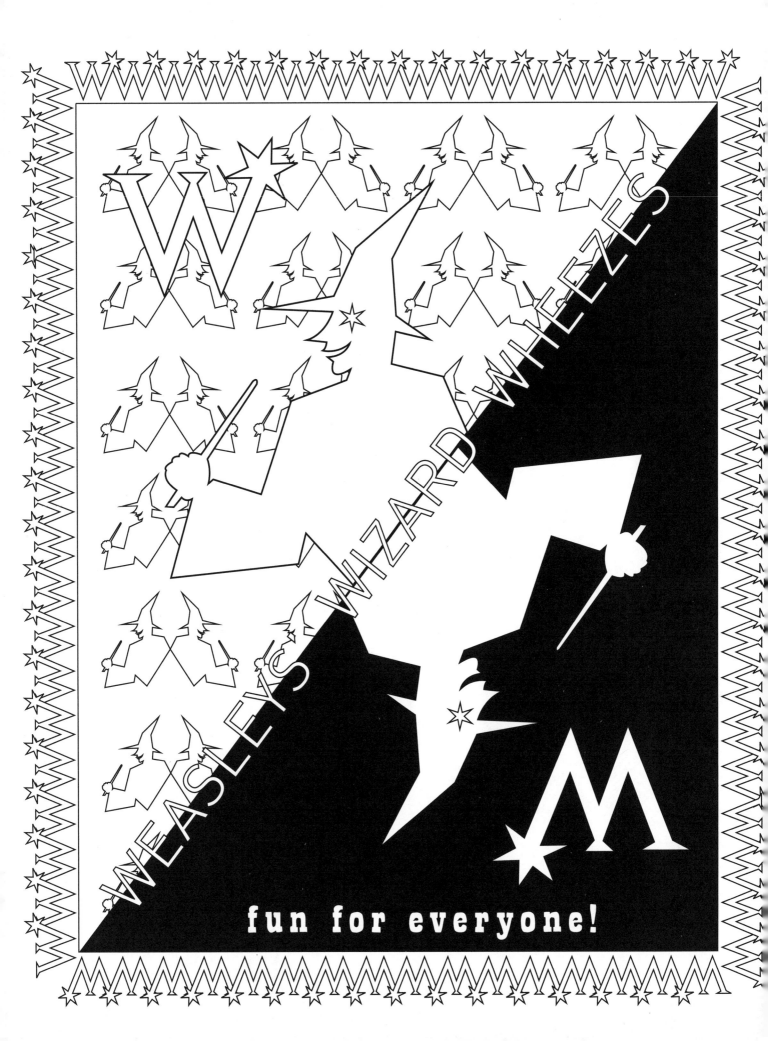

THE

№ 24027 · The Wizarding World's Alternative Voice

QUIBBLER

PANDEMONIUM at THE MINISTRY

"WHAT A PALAVER!"

BY X. LOVEGOOD / pg.7

POP OUT HERE!

WRACKSPURTS

UNFUZZ THE MYSTERY PG12

EXCLUSIVE "MY WEEK WITHOUT RUNES!"

PG24

BREAKING NEWS

FISHWIVES FINALLY GRANTED EQUAL RIGHTS PG 30

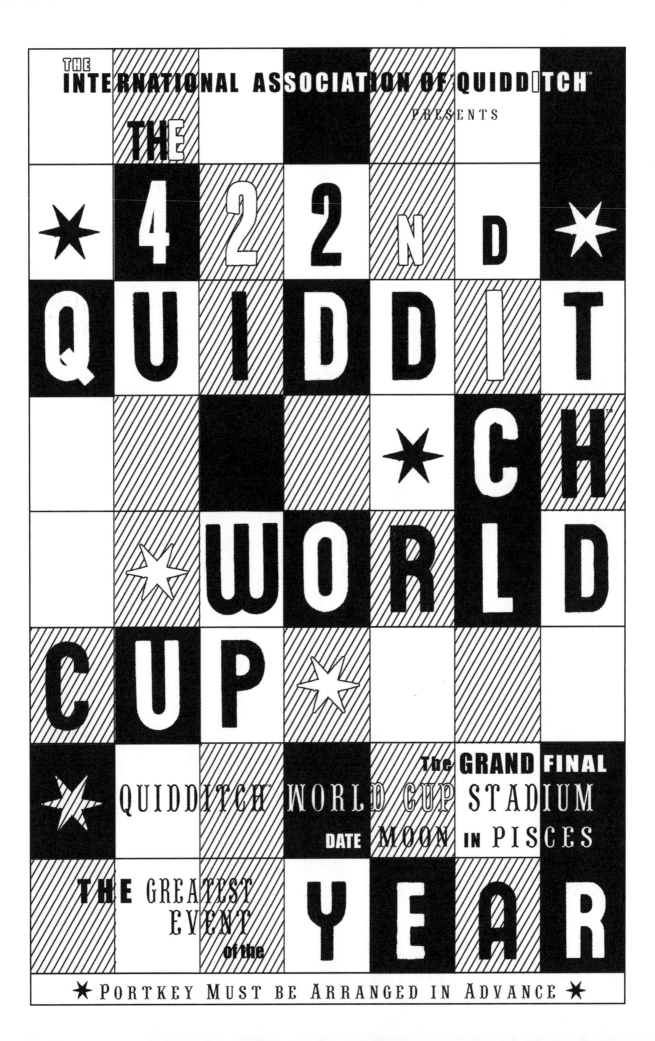

THE CREATURES AND BEASTS

of the wizarding world are majestic and funny,
chilling and loving. They are as diverse a group of
characters as the students who attend Hogwarts School
of Witchcraft and Wizardry, and just as much a part
of the magic of the Harry Potter films. The pages that
follow present a selection of the fauna from the films
and invite you to reimagine the fiery red feathers of
Fawkes, the ghostly hues of the merpeople, the
weathered scales of dragons—and so much more.

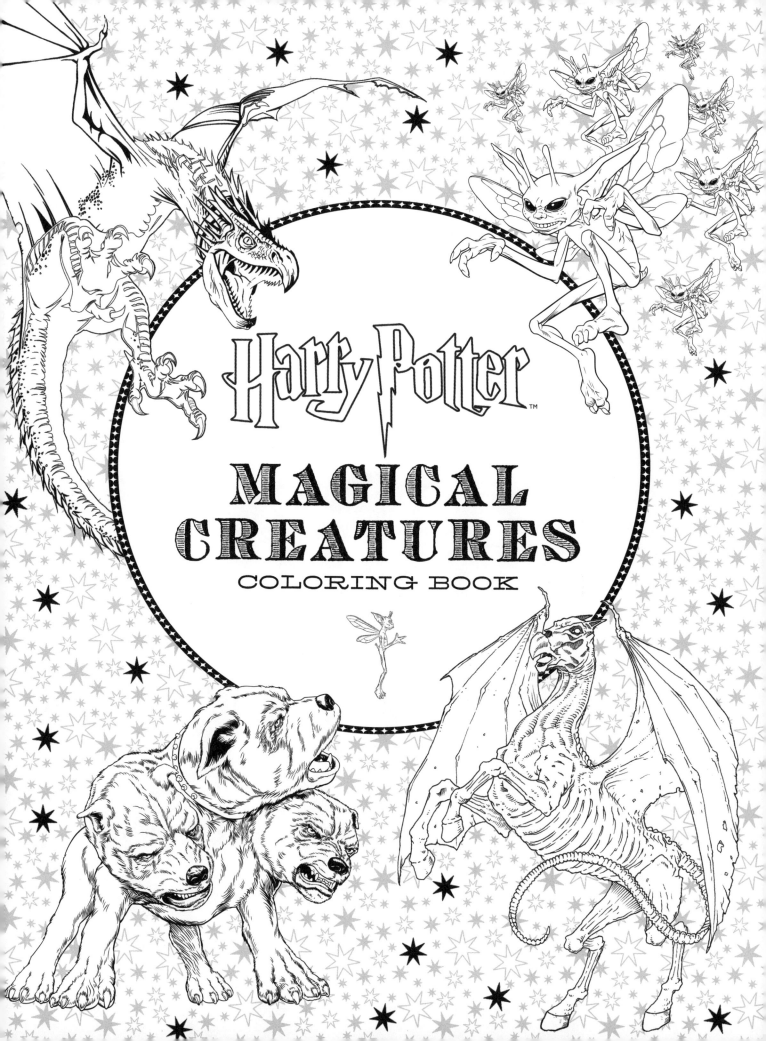

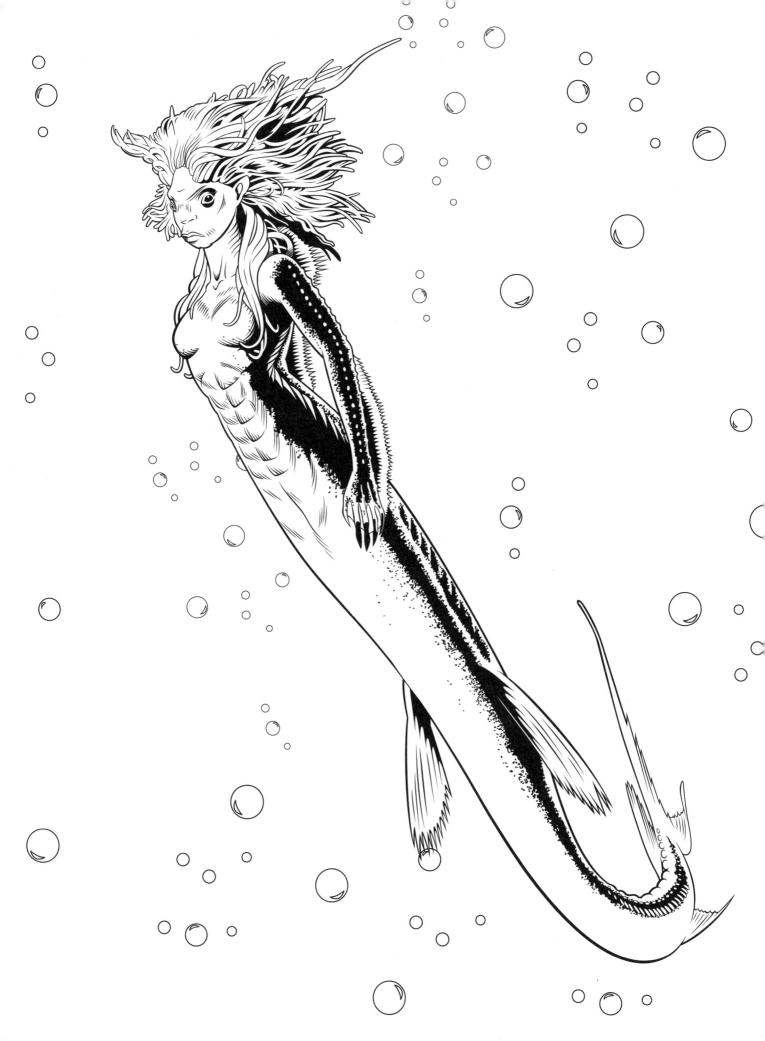

he world we journey through in the Harry Potter films is magical and extraordinary. From a bank run by goblins to a castle filled with staircases that move, we are continually taken to new and incredible places. We follow a young boy who has discovered a world he never knew existed and we encounter there a thrilling cast of wizards, witches— and so much more. The pages that follow are an invitation to relive the magic of the Harry Potter films and bring your own vibrant colors to the wizarding world outlined here in black and white.

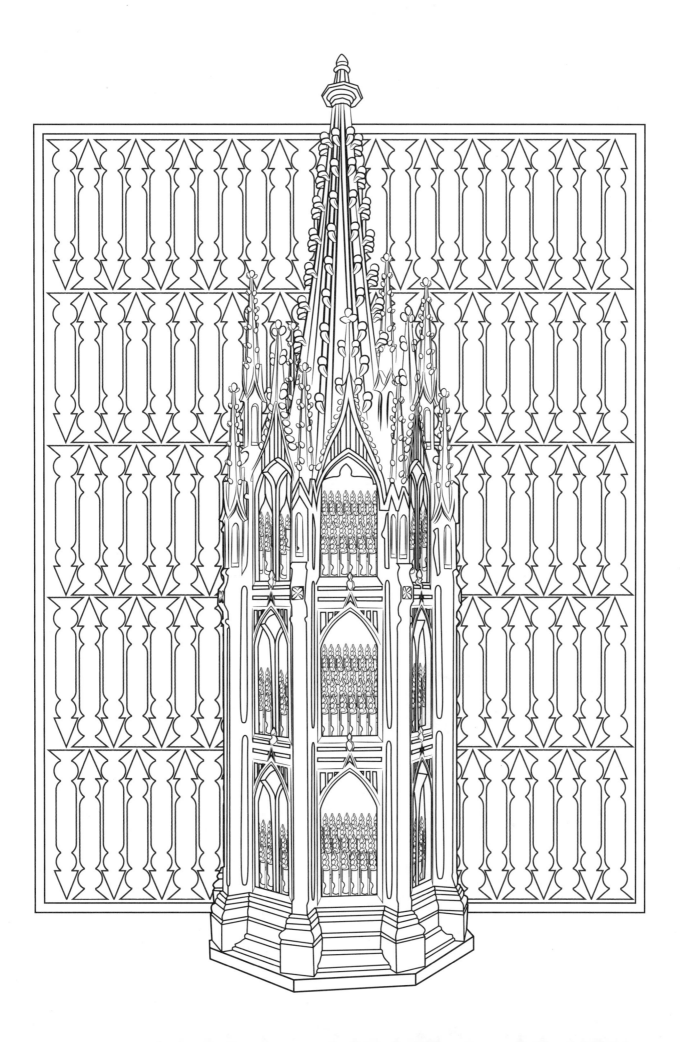

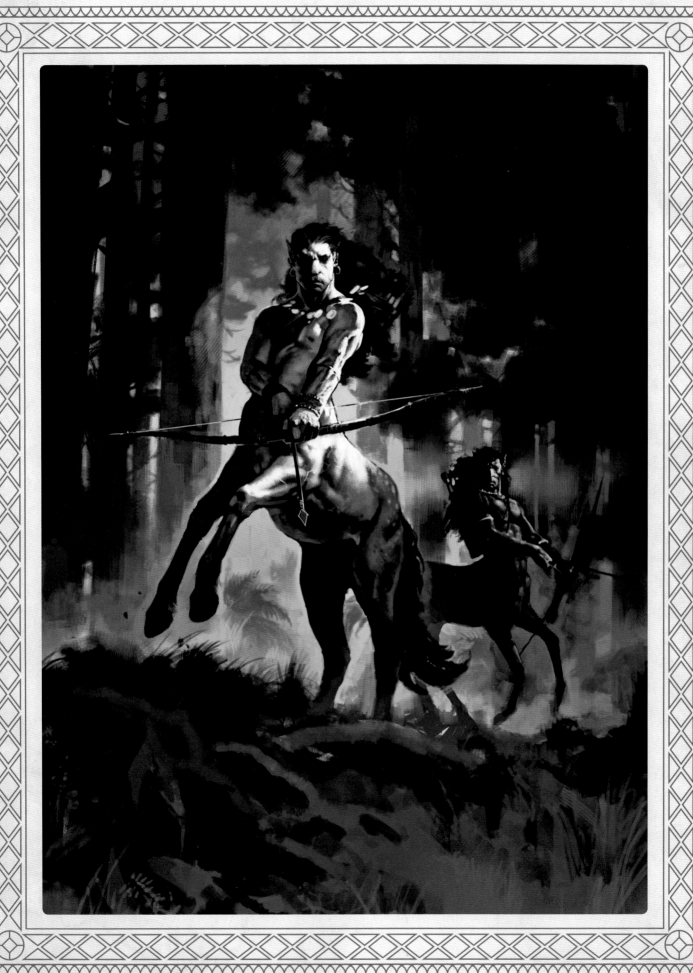

THE
INTERNATIONAL ASSOCIATION OF QUIDDITCH

PRESENTS

THE
422ND
QUIDDITCH
WORLD
CUP

The **GRAND** FINAL
QUIDDITCH WORLD CUP STADIUM
DATE MOON IN PISCES

THE GREATEST EVENT of the **YEAR**

PORTKEY MUST BE ARRANGED IN ADVANCE

PRODUCED BY

PO Box 3088
San Rafael, CA 94912
www.insighteditions.com

PUBLISHER: Raoul Goff
ART DIRECTOR: Chrissy Kwasnik
JUNIOR DESIGNER: Leah Bloise
EXECUTIVE EDITOR: Vanessa Lopez
PROJECT EDITOR: Greg Solano
PRODUCTION EDITOR: Rachel Anderson
PRODUCTION MANAGER: Lina s Palma
PRODUCTION COORDINATOR: Pauline Kerkhove Sellin

INSIGHT EDITIONS would like to thank Victoria Selover,
Elaine Piechowski, and Melanie Swartz.

ILLUSTRATIONS BY Adam Raiti, Robin F. Williams, Maxime Lebrun,
Dee Pei, Frans Boukas, Britt Wilson, and Manuel Martinez.

Insight Editions, in association with Roots of Peace, will plant two
trees for each tree used in the manufacturing of this book. Roots of
Peace is an internationally renowned humanitarian organization
dedicated to eradicating land mines worldwide and converting
war-torn lands into productive farms and wildlife habitats. Roots
of Peace will plant two million fruit and nut trees in Afghanistan
and provide farmers there with the skills and support necessary for
sustainable land use.

Manufactured in the United States by Insight Editions

10 9 8 7 6 5 4 3